THE ONLY WORLD

THE ONLY WORLD

POEMS BY

LYNDA HULL

Edited with a foreword by David Wojahn

HarperPerennial
A Division of HarperCollins*Publishers*

HarperCollins books may be purchased for educational, business, or sales promotional use. For information please write: Special Markets Department, HarperCollins Publishers, Inc., 10 East 53rd Street, New York, NY 10022.

FIRST EDITION

Designed by Gloria Adelson/Lulu Graphics

ISBN 0-06-055363-4
ISBN 0-06-095112-5 (pbk.)

95 96 97 98 99 ❖/HC 10 9 8 7 6 5 4 3 2 1

Acknowledgment is made to the following journals, in which these poems first appeared:

The American Voice	"Chiffon"
Colorado Review	"Red Velvet Jacket"
Crazyhorse	"Rivers into Seas"
	"Denouement"
Denver Quarterly	"River Bridge"
The Iowa Review	"Fortunate Traveller"
	"Amulets"
Indiana Review	"Bar Xanadu"
	"Street of Crocodiles"
The Kenyon Review	"Suite for Emily"
New England	
Review	"Fiat Lux"
	"The Window"
Ploughshares	"Ornithology"
Pushcart Prize XIX:	
Best of the Small	
Presses	"Suite for Emily"
Red Brick Review	"At the Westland"
Third Coast	"For Ann"

Thanks are also due to the National Endowment for the Arts and the Illinois Arts Council for fellowships that aided the completion of this collection.

Contents

Foreword

There was no poet of her generation who possessed greater lyric gifts than Lynda Hull; nor was there a poet who wrote more harrowingly. This combination helped to create an astonishing body of work, and the poems of *The Only World* show a writer who is working at the height of her considerable powers.

When Lynda died in an auto accident in March 1994, she had hoped in the coming months to arrange the poems collected here for publication. It then fell to me to structure the book. As her husband of ten years, I was fortunate to have been the first to read, critique, and help edit the poems of her three books. And Lynda returned this favor by serving as the first—and always the best and most unsparing—reader and critic of my own poems. Surely the structure and selection of poems of *The Only World* is not precisely that which Lynda would have envisioned. But in the last months of her life I had numerous conversations with her about the arrangement and possible titles for the book that was emerging, and my structure for the book attempts to reflect her wishes.

Posthumously published books such as this invariably are seen as memento mori, read as a variety of elegy rather than as the sort of urgent and vital confrontation with the lived life that Lynda demanded from herself and her poems. Although Lynda's poetry is characterized always by its unflinching look at mortality and the manifold losses, both personal and historical, which are our lot in these times, the ferocity of her poems comes not from sorrow and defeatism but from a hard-won and urgently expressed spirit of wonder. And it is this quality, more than anything else, that makes me believe her poems will find readers for many years to come. Although these poems acknowledge a world that Lynda saw as "burning ruthless, cruel and exacting," it is also, and more importantly, a world Lynda Hull refused to be bowed by. These are poems that offer—in the words of her favorite writer, Hart Crane—"the unbetrayable reply/ whose accent no farewell can know."

DAVID WOJAHN

I

Chiffon

Fever, down-right dirty sweat
   of a heat-wave in May turning everyone
      pure body. Back of knee, cleavage, each hidden

crease, nape of neck turning steam. Deep
   in last night's vast factory, the secret
      wheels that crank the blue machinery

of weather bestowed this sudden cool,
   the lake misting my morning walk, this
      vacant lot lavish with iris—saffron,

indigo, bearded and striated, a shock
   of lavender clouds among shattered brick
      like cumulus that sail the tops of highrises

clear evenings. Surprising as the iris garden
   I used to linger in, a girl distant from me
      now as a figure caught in green glass,

an oasis gleamed cool with oval plaques
   naming blooms Antoinette, My Blue Sunset,
      Festival Queen. This morning's iris frill

damp as fabulous gowns after dancing,
   those rummage sale evening gowns church ladies
      gave us another hot spring, 1967.

JoAnn who'd soon leave school, 14, pregnant,
  Valerie with her straightened bouffant hair.
    That endless rooftop season before the panic

and sizzle, the torched divided cities,
  they called me *cousin on the light side.*
    Camphorous, awash in rusty satin rosettes,

in organdy, chiffon, we'd practice
  girl group radio-hits—Martha Reeves
    but especially Supremes—JoAnn vamping

Diana, me and Valerie doing Flo and Mary's
  background moans, my blonde hair pinned
    beneath Jo's mother's Sunday wig.

The barest blue essence of Evening in Paris
  scented our arms. We perfected all the gestures,
    JoAnn's liquid hands sculpting air,

her fingers' graceful cupping, wrist turning,
  palm held flat, "Stop in the Name of Love,"
    pressing against the sky's livid contrails,

a landscape flagged with laundry, tangled
  aerials and billboards, the blackened
    railway bridges and factories ruinous

in their fumes. Small hand held against the flood
  of everything to come, the savage drifting years.
    I'm a lucky bitch. Engulfed in the decade's riotous

swells, that lovely gesture, the dress, plumage
  electrifying the fluid force of that young body.
    She was gang-raped later that year. The rest,

4

as they say, *is history.* History.
 When I go back I pore the phone book for names
  I'll never call. Peach Pavilion, Amethyst

Surprise. *Cousin on the light side.* Bend
 to these iris, their piercing ambrosial
  essence, the heart surprised, dark and bitter.

Red Velvet Jacket

It's almost Biblical driving this midnight burning highway
past South Bronx exits
with the names of streets once known, where torched cars
spiral columns
acetylene blue & white. We're in the universe of lost things
where the lights are out,
the lamp pawned & soon the record player, that enamelled
  table,
clothes, the rooms & faces,

air hissing soft through the rolled-down window like
silk velvet slipping hot
into my handbag, velvet fine as a fingerprint whorl,
maroon as the long dusty cars
that sharked these avenues, mildewed upholstery like
it was always raining night,
the insides ripped out of everything. But I was talking
about the red velvet jacket

that hangs even now in the mind flaring its slow veronicas
in recollection's wind that breathes
the mineral glamour of cornices & pilasters, districts
that burned years ago.
These days at the fringes even trains turn express,
the bombed-out blocks & clustered faces
blurred featureless. Out of sight, out of mind. Midnight's
burning highway, another charred strip-job.

Recollection: gather back the gleaming fragments & Warsaw
  flashes

a museum model of the Ghetto—
the Jews immured, a system of catwalks and barricades,
the trams' blackened windows
so that citizens might blindly pass, might invent consoling
    fictions.
Columns of flame light now
this tangled graffiti to a kind of incantation.
Called back in wonder,

the strangeness, the story endlessly told any life unfurls,
causal chains of small decisions,
almost random, those accidents of grace or luck. That red velvet
'30s jacket. How it sleeked
over the hips, elaborate glass buttons, how it made me feel
a little dangerous, a sense
of stolen fortune or history, as if I'd been chosen
for extraordinary moments, as if

I'd walk untouched, fire parting smoothly before me, liquid
& blue, that refused to singe,
to mar the bearer with a scar to signify the event.
Red velvet the color
of that long car we'd cruise under the river through
    Alphabetown,
then the Bronx, Hunts Point
& its flooded streets awash with crates of rotting fruit,
streets that figure still

relentless in the endless anarchy of dreams—
the Puerto Rican dealer, Juan, his wife, the kid. (Shift the car
to 5th, don't stop,
don't slow down.) But the door splinters all over again.
The jump-the-dealer routine.
Red velvet sleeve rolled up, snake of blue vein, snake

of salsa rising from the streets,
the warmth sexual, turning me capable, the grain of the wood

on the floor flowering into the music, each fiber,
each splinter, until the tree
it came from greened in the mind. No, it's the watery
green of neon flickering
the boy's face by the window, the baby in his arms dangling
over the street, the mother screaming.
His faced striped green & blue & the water of the neon
stutters turning Spanish

on my tongue. *Darme, darme el niño.* Accidental grace.
I just wanted the screaming to stop.
Someone muffles the mother, but he's watching me—sole white
    face,
blanched translucent—& across his face
all the complexity a gaze can be. Calculation at first, fear,
disdain, the crying child. And what
did he see? Some hopped-up 16 year old with police-colored
    skin.

God I was innocent then, clean as a beast in the streets.
At the fringes of Warsaw's Ghetto
stands a prison where they sorted Jews from politicals,
politicals from homosexuals,
where masses dispersed to nameless erasure. There's a tree
    there,
lopped & blackened, yet it shines,
enshrined in prayer scrolls, nailed icons. Oh, lucky life,
I didn't understand until tonight,

called back from the ruins in that jacket, dark stain blooming
through the sleeve, the child squalling
in my useless arms. I don't know what happened to the jacket

& all those people are lost to a diaspora,
the borough incinerated around them, nowhere in this night
I drive through. Silk velvet and its rich hiss
the shade of flame offering its drapery, its charm
against this world burning ruthless, crucial & exacting.

Ornithology

Gone to seed, ailanthus, the poverty
   tree. Take a phrase, then
fracture it, the pods' gaudy nectarine shades
     ripening to parrots taking flight, all crest
and tail feathers.
              A musical idea.
                     Macaws

   scarlet and violet,
                  tangerine as a song
the hue of sunset where my street becomes water

and down shore this phantom city skyline's
   mere hazy silhouette. The alto's
liquid geometry weaves *a way of thinking,*
     a way of breaking
synchronistic
             through time
                     so the girl

  on the corner
           has the bones of my face,
the old photos, beneath the Kansas City hat,

black fedora lifting hair off my neck
   cooling the sweat of a night-long tidal
pull from bar to bar the night we went
     to find Bird's grave. Eric's chartreuse
perfume. That
            poured-on dress
                  I lived days

and nights inside,
                    made love
and slept in, a mesh and slur of zipper

down the back. Women smoked the boulevards
    with gardenias afterhours, asphalt shower-
slick, ozone charging air with sixteenth
        notes, that endless convertible ride to find
the grave
            whose sleep and melody
                            wept neglect
        enough to torch us
                    for a while
through snare-sweep of broom on pavement,

the rumpled musk of lover's sheets, charred
    cornices topping crosstown gutted buildings.
Torches us still—cat screech, matte blue steel
        of pistol stroked across the victim's cheek
where fleet shoes
                    jazz this dark
                            and peeling
        block, that one.
                    Vine Street, Olive.
We had the music, but not the pyrotechnics—

rhinestone straps lashing my shoes, heels sinking
    through earth and Eric in casual drag,
mocha cheekbones rouged, that flawless
        plummy mouth. A style for moving,
heel tap and
            lighter flick,
                    lion moan
        of buses pulling away
                        through the static
brilliant fizz of taffeta on nyloned thighs.

Light mist, etherous, rinsed our faces
　　and what happens when
you touch a finger to the cold stone
　　　that jazz and death played
down to?
　　　　　Phrases.
　　　　　　　Take it all
　　and break forever—
　　　　　　　　　a man
with gleaming sax, an open sill in summertime,

and the fire-escape's iron zigzag tumbles
　　crazy notes to a girl cooling her knees,
wearing one of those dresses no one wears
　　　anymore, darts and spaghetti straps, glitzy
fabrics foaming
　　　　　　an iron bedstead.
　　　　　　　　　　The horn's
　　alarm, then fluid brass chromatics.
　　　　　　　　　　Extravagant
ailanthus, the courtyard's poverty tree is spike
and wing, slate-blue
　　　　　　mourning dove,
　　　　　　　　　sudden cardinal flame.

If you don't live it, it won't come out your horn.

Fiat Lux

Static from the radio stippled grey as anesthesia dream,
band after band of voices,
the luminous bar of speedometer, column shift. Cruising,
the long battered car fogged
in whiskey breath, the sumptuous trash, canvas scraps, pasteled
bills of lading. Father and daughter—

and over them blue spruce laden with snow arcing the white
mansioned avenue of robber barons'
palaces, the steamship magnates and celebrities, the city's
skyline gothamed electric
across the horizon. Small hands on the pane wick the chill
until I'm icy pure flame,

outside the big houses, streets unwinding below like a tulle
    scarf
from a woman's shoulders
to the damp wooden houses huddled in their steam, the
    marshes'
smoking blackness beyond. Swallow the moon like a coin,
an ivory poker chip polished

for luck, driving fast past the opera singer's house, his name
like nervous laughter, that
music blown to shards, arias of ice, and always the city's
dragon-back silhouette, someplace
a child might never get to. *Fiat lux,* the windows'
glow, buttery and old.

The city's become a figure for the way you've learned to love
what's distant, fantastic,
an abyss of space between. One of those returning things,
    skeins
of planetary days, lunar phases,
solar years turning harmonies celestial in the blood. One's
never done with the past.

Close your eyes. The laden winter night, hill tumbling down
and beneath the burning meadows'
spreading stain, the runaway's smoking train through roots, the
    blind
white worms and rat swarms
underneath the mercury-colored river. I always loved stories
that began that way: the elaborate entry

to the city of cast-iron garlands and window displays intricate
as a universe with shining cogs
and wheels, a world where night reversed to day, and towering
    women
waterfalled their Dynel tresses
in the shelter of marquees, boas spitting plumage in the faces
of nightwaiters.

Yes, the gilded birds, plunder in the turrets. And the pulse,
the mission, secret formulas
discovered all around me, the daughter swept in her black
    serge
dust-bin coat, tangled in foxtails,
glass eyes, shoplifter's pockets sewn inside stuffed with broken
    trinkets,
cancelled stamps from Peru and Mozambique.

Fingers tracing the skyline through the windshield of that
    battered car:

mere *fiat lux,* tricks,
delusions of sleek verb, the lustrous nouns. How to imagine
those places where chaos
holds sway, the old night where you hear scared laughter
    pierce
the anesthesia dream, song

of shoulders pushed rough to alley walls, torn caress, dark
    dress,
song that goes
I'll do it for 10, for 5, I'll do it, burnt spoon twisted in the pocket.
Don't tell her. Child stroking
the frosted pane, galactic, impervious and caught in this endless
coming to be that's endlessly undone,

the long car's weaving tracks blurred quickly in the snow
    beneath
the laden shelter of trees,
my father's whiskied breath as we drove like thieves through
    skeins
of planetary nights, air rich
with signals, the arias and perfect boundless schemes where
the city floated
distant and celestial, brutal in its own rung music.

Amulets

Riddled by seaworms, the figurehead's blind
unsurprised eyes gaze past a tattooed sailor's
hide, brindled with waves & fish, spreadeagled
on the wall, this coastal town museum. Clumsy
dioramas, ivory birdcages, the instruments of

celestial navigation. Down gallery,
in her battered leather jacket, I watch Emily
& her daughter kneel to spy through miniature
isinglass windows. An immense dollhouse:
each parlor, bedroom & hallway opening to

surprise, a mansion of possibility, each
salver & bannister burnished to perfection.
The latest t-cell count report crumpled
in her pocket, she points to a tiny
muslin gown draping a chair as if just shrugged

from someone's shoulders freshly risen from
sleep's farthest shore, the shapes that flit
there—a man scarified with tidal waves
& floral demons, a harpy carved to plunge
like a diving horse from the ship's prow

through an ocean of ice. I need some amulet,
those charms we made as girls of locks
scissored from each other's hair
because mere faith did not seem harbor enough
in a world of brute possibility.

Or these pendants & bracelets woven entirely
of human hair. Storms of it—chestnut,
auburn, eternally growing, blue-sheened black,
ashen blonde pulled from brushes, combs, soaked
& dried, combed & knotted, shellacked

with yellow sealing wax. Talismans.
The ill-typed card of explanation warps
through the glass case, currents & bubbles
rippling the whirr of voices diminuendoed
when I close my eyes to watch, like vision,

half-remembered, pulled from dream,
black mares beneath their plumes dragging
a cortege, crepe-hung, through heavy pearled
sands, a stinging hiss of ocean swallowing
one more name, some pestilence, women

letting down storms of wavy hair, though it's only
a sepiaed photo I'm recalling, Grandmother
& her sisters with their jewel names,
Opal, Ruby, Sapphire, posed in a parlor
for tableaux vivants—the Graces

with their billowing knee-length tresses, loose
white gowns, but I should have thought of them
as Fates, the trio set afloat beyond
the farthest shores lofting pearl-handled scissors
against whole skeins of thread. Galeforce winds

rattle locks, breathe ragged around the walls
like black horses laboring through sand, fears
given form, phantoms a child might magically
appease. We did it all wrong. Emily, who says
she's never felt looked over, never been

protected, or spared. What I hear is
her laughter, the child's long aspirant *ahhh*
of wonder. What I need is some talisman, an amulet,
the old cosmology with its crystalline
perfection of shells around the world, celestial

frictive music to navigate by. Who'd want
to surrender? Skies pearled cold, the sea's
lullaby crooned in the shell of the ear,
I know, the houses scrawled by moonlight
down the hill, salted around the bay frozen

to filigree, smooth floes of ice. Nervous
hands twisting, Emily braids her long hair,
rich as a mare's tail cascading, scars
mapping each vein with the addict's tattoo:
her immune system's failing.

How do I place them standing like figures
in a glass case, shore's edge where sand pearls
beneath the dome of stars—a world
safe & comprehensible? How is a spell woven,
like these jewels, through the hours' twilit progress?

Braids ovalling silhouettes meant for wearing
like holy medals against bare skin. Starbursts,
whorls inspiralled as the heart of a nebula,
charms meant to cheat fate, to stay the journeyer
a little while longer, who'll never pass this way again.

River Bridge

Winter, stepping into the night trolley,
quarter pint of scotch in pocket . . . *No not that one.*
The childhood story—Grandmother reading among
her violets a poem about the elevated train
slithering its worm down London's spine.
Not that one. I could tell you skeins
of train stories, as now through this dense
summer night, trees swarming green their canopy
over the street of warm lit windows, the train
slashes its path through the neighborhood, whirr
and pulse, the heart and fuse of distance filling
the room, hurtling through countless frames,
the scenes—now that curtainless room of young men
preening shirtless before their mirrors, now
the ward of iron hospital beds. *I've seen them.*
By the screen, the white cat swivels her ears
to follow the train until it's lost in glass
smashing, the alley voices. Who's walking tonight?
Who's hungry? The story I keep returning to
is the one about walking hungry over
that St. Louis railroad bridge. *Why that one?*
Is it the bridge? Bridge linking one riverbank aflame
in smokestacks, the slaughterhouses, to
the bank where the city's glittering Andromeda
spilled itself before them. Bridge
of flying hands and curses, iron bridge
and the passage of colliers, boxcars, the gondolas

freighting coal, dull sprockets,
sleek carriages of lingerie and crystal.

Distant, the sceptered city glints, a figment,
I could begin. Or *once, there was a time,*
the opening a fairy tale, simple, sinister.

II

January, its savage tempers & mirthless
North wind have iced the iron bridges' spans.
Between flaming riverbanks, the two walk thin
as flame, a world refined to fierce purity—
lungs blued to filigree, bare ankle, damp sleeve
frosted beneath the other's steadying hand.
Stepping tie to tie,
the river churned below
its suicide babble, the nitrous drowned
sopranos, sulfuric moans. Such a grand manner
of entry, fareless, in stealth,
the city's lit gateway fuming like midnight's
wild schemes. Should I ask the obvious questions?
Such as what was the engine driving the machine
of their travel? Oh, fear, that's familiar. Folly,
leavened recklessly with hope. Lights multiply
against the sky, the city's slow Andromeda,
a constellation the shape of what they seek,
the streets *inside* of Berlined facades, people
breakfasting in mid-air, walls torn down. The squatter's
palace. The rat's domain, each moment rinsed
in benzine, sharpened with amphetamine,
the hunger. Alluvial voices
hissing beneath them *dogs of chaos,*
escape from the burning city, no time, no time.

The river knows the story. The get-out-of-town-fast story.
A dizzy trip through the ripped underside of things—
that rough fugitive coinage, begged rides,
begged meals. Somebody fed us. Somebody said
get out of town. Those E. St. Louis backyards sooty
with frozen laundry trees. Should I say the Mississippi knows
the story of the room left behind, the bad deals?
Like a scene playing out in a glass globe
I might hold in my palm, I can watch them:
oh look at those fools, the cold carving
them up to some version of bewildered miracle.

III

Deep freeze humming the rails, the entrance
into the unknown city, the bus station pulsing
fluorescent waves across ranks of pay tvs,
a quarter a view for those laying over, for those
mired in dim rooms, too long alone with themselves.
You know how it is. The fact of death starts pearling
large in the mind, darkening its banks of offices,
ballrooms where you might touch some face
you recognize, those staircases that spiral, collapse
amidst the body's mysteries, its harsh betrayals.
Or love's betrayals. Through static, the P.A. spits
destinations, frayed galaxies of names—*Columbus,*
Joplin, St. Joe, Points West, Kansas City. . . .
How does one thing part from another? Redrawing tendrils
& roots, a lopped amputation that leaves this one
raving in the street, the other cold, cold . . .
alone in the room after such intensity, the way
it would be, me leaving E. so crassly after
the crazy journey. I think now I've become
a character in this, must slip on the coat,

these salt-wet shoes, sip the raw whiskey
and in the drunken radiance the tvs spill
over sleepers' faces hear the late-night tapdancers,
the anthems & jets. Then the station signal's
high bat-cry peeling away to the automated
voice, *Chicago, Detroit, Points North.* . . .
After the parting, one from the other, there's
the long reclamation, flood plain, phantom
limb. From one form to another: transit.

IV

Oh, the anarchy of owning nothing
but a constellation the shape of what they seek.
The get-out-of-town-fast story. No bus fare,
and where to go
in this steaming plenty, the lit kitchens
& parlors glimpsed from the street washed
citron by lamplight. Is it the stolen car
again in this version, or the abandoned movie palace?
I can put them in the theater and show them
making love, warm with each other
& the begged bottle of scotch & they can sleep
in mouldering velvets. Stripped bare,
sapphired in blue air, she'd be a woman served
to the city's glittering Andromeda.
Like the Russian cellist broke in Berlin,
the '20s, who'd sleep in the opera house, who
one delirious night played, naked, his instrument
into the shadows, the banked silent seats
& rat galleries. And forgot the cold.
That would be pretty wouldn't it?
But the theater's barricaded, and so,
it must be, as it always is, the stolen car.

Beyond the city it will spirit them
into the blizzard, the etherous drifts, until
the engine stops & the road erases, trackless.
And then she'll know ice needling the blood
to scarlet foliage. But, how to show the calm
when she thinks, *so this is what it's like to die,*
a twisting bolt of black cloth dragged back
through stations, the bare dusty rooms, chalk dust
& sachet, the river's voices
deep nitrous green. How calm. Pocking snow
on the windshield, heavy and damp as the voices
of crows in her grandmother's trees,
a cry she mimicked at the back of her throat,
harsh and wild. White crows
now blessing her eyes. How calm.

V

When the authorities lifted them away
from there, they entered a world of steam,
that fallen roadside constellation chromed
with coffee urns, galaxies of white plates.
Crossing the bridge back, again, the blood's
fierce arterial surge like arias, like
alarming camellias scarlet with snow
still frosting the ground. Heavy and warm,
cups of coffee steamed in our hands, the good
bitter coffee. But always, we were aware,
hear still, the pulse and singing:
I am the stranger coiled on the landing, singing
this is the bridge of the flying hands,
the mansion of the body. I am the one
who scratched at your door, the one who begged
rough coinage. This is the blessing

& this a hymnal of wings. Hear the heart's
greedy alluvial choir, a cascading train
whirring the tracks: called back,
called back from the river.

VI

Chirring in her throat the white cat stretches
on the sill, all ruffled ivory, present-tense,
muscular pure. Can one possess a clear vision
of oneself in the world? Dominion over
all that bewildering wrack? This raised hand
against the evening's towering cream and smoke
conjures a flurry of ghost hands, a crowd
glimpsed blurred from the hurtling train. Clouds
billow & unknot a sudden shower releasing
that lavish wet asphalt perfume, the fragrance
of countless showers over scores of cities, each one
intensely *now, now, this sweet wrenched only.*
From the turbulent river, moments swim unbidden
to the surface, others never rise at all, the lost
drowned arias, sunken avenues of camphored rooms,
the walls with their watery initials. Phantom
destinations, the P.A.'s *St. Joe, Kansas City,*
Denver, points beyond the laden plains surging
beneath waves of snow, blue perilous mountains,
locales in the mind.
The cat leaps, again a train, striking this time
a smooth oiled chord, as if there might be
singing on the other side of the tracks.
Some Jordan. That otherness, those secret times,
the bridges beneath the surface of a life.
Pull on the rough coat and salt-wet shoes.
Let the liquor burn your throat. Did I do that?

Could that have been me? Those figures crossing
the bridge, setting out, always setting out.
Voices I must keep listening for in these sharpening
leaves, among the stacks and flames,
the smoking pillars. *Someone fed them.*
Someone said get out of town.

II

Suite for Emily

1. The Letter

Everywhere the windows give up nothing
but frost's intricate veined foliage.
Just engines shrilling pocked and frozen streets
wailing towards some new disaster.
No *bright* angels' ladders going to split
heaven this Chicago instant where the pier's
an iced fantastic: spiked, the glacial floes
seize it greedy like a careless treasure—

marquise diamonds, these round clear globes, the psychic's
crystal world spinning in her corner shop
when I passed, a globe boundaried with turning
silent winds and demons. Out here the pavement's
a slick graffitied strip: *There's more to life
than violence.* Someone's added *Yes, Sex and Drugs.*
Hello, Plague Angel. I just heard your wings
hiss off the letter on my table—Emily's

in prison again, her child's lost to the State,
Massachusetts. Fatigue, pneumonia,
the wasting away. In the secret hungering,
the emptiness when we were young would come
the drug's good sweep like nothing else,
godly almost the way we'd float immune
& couldn't nothing touch us, nothing.
Somehow I'd thought you'd pass her over—

positive yes—but never really sick,
that flayed above her door there'd be some sign
of mercy. But there's only January's
rough ministry peeling my face away.
Light like the cruel light of another century
& I'm thinking of Dickinson's letter
"Many who were in their bloom have gone
to their last account and the mourners go about

the streets." The primer pages yellowing
on her shelf beneath an album of pressed gentian:
"Do most people live to be old? No, one half die
before they are eight years old. But one in four lives
to see twenty-one." She'd known the bitter sponge
pressed to the fevered forehead, the Death Angel's
dark familiar company, how she'd swirl her veils,
how she'd lean over the ewer and basin

blackening the water. This arctic water, this
seething rustle—lamé, sequins, a glitter wrap
trailing from a girl's shoulders so the shadow pimps
go *hey princess, why you so sad tonight,*
let me make you happy, when she's only tired,
up all night & needing a hit to let her sleep.
We know that story, the crest and billow
and foam and fleeting fullness

before the disappearing. Discs of hissing ice,
doors you (I?) might fall through to the underworld
of bars & bus stations, private rooms of
dancing girls numb-sick & cursing the wilderness
of men's round blank faces. Spinning demons.
Round spoon of powder hissing over the flame.
Worlds within worlds, beneath worlds, worlds that flare
and consume so they become the only world.

2. Holy City, City of Night

What is that general rule which tells
  how long a thing will live? The primer answers,
Whatever grows quick decays quick: soon ripe,
  soon rotten. The rust-blown calla gracing
my table, those Boston girls 20 years gone,
young men in lace & glitter washed alien
  by gasoline sunsets, the burning sphere
lapsing below night's black rim. *Live fast, die . . .*

we know the rest. Reckless anthem.
  The pier cable's ice-sleeved beneath
my hands—miraculous, yes, to be here
  januaried by this lake's barbaric winterscape
Dickinson might read as savage text
& emblem of a deity indifferent. Her embassy lay
  beyond the city of jasper & gold, the beaten
wrought towers scripture promised the saved

would enter. What heaven she found she made.
  And so did we, worlds that sear, consume—earthly,
delirious. *Ignis fatuus.* Strike the match,
  the fizzing cap. But Oh Reader, the wild beauty
of it, the whirring rush, blonde hiss of aerial
miles, worn stairways in every burning school
  of nodding classrooms, the buzz-snap of
talk blurring hallucinatory fraught

avenues. Illusive inner city, drugged
  majestic residence spiralled with staircases,
balustrades rococoed, lapidary. Invisible empires
  dreamt beneath the witchery of birds
circling the Common with twilight, their caw
& settle, the patterns as they wheel

over the pond's reflective mirror bruised
roseate, violet, deeper, the swanboats

darkening into night's charged dazzle,
   Park Square joints gone radiant, the bus station
burnished before the zap, the charge, the edge.
   It was the life wasn't it? Compatriots you'd
just love to die for, who'd jump you
in a New York minute. But the glory
   as the lights went up, torching the air chartreuse,
lipsticked pink, casting embers, seraphic fires

fallen earthward. Fallen, the furious emblems.
   We were so young we'd spend & spend
ourselves as if there'd be no reckoning, then grew
   past caring. All the darkening chapters.
Dream time, the inner time
where towers and battlements erect
   their coruscating glamour & how we'd glide,
celebrities among them, the crowds falling back,

dream deeper, gone & wake to daylight's assault
   knocking another bare room, the alley, the bathroom
you inhabit like the thief you are. *Ignis fatuus.*
   I can follow you there, Emily, we girls
setting out a thousand ruined nights in the splendor
of the torched & reckless hour.
   Who wouldn't trade heaven for that fleet city
when winter beaks the shattered pane,

when summer's a nauseous shimmer
   of sexual heat, though sex is a numb machine
you float above? When the place you walk into
   is a scream in the shape of yourself.
When it makes perfect sense to blow someone away

for 20 bucks beyond even your bleak human universe.
    When the only laughter that falls down
is iron & godless. Here, I—the one who left—

must falter where persists
    this chrome traffic shrill, where the cable's
bitter alloy comes away in my hand,
    this metalled pungence of hair and skin
in wind persists riven as the taste of myself,
the blood blooming healthy,
    real in my mouth, a future's lavish venues
spread stunned before me. These hands.

3. COMBAT ZONE/WAR STORIES

The district's been demolished, sown with salt.
The dazzling girls, girls, girls in platinum wigs
have been lifted away by some infernal agency,
the queens, exotic Amazons & rough-trade gay boys.

Sometimes I go back to walk the streets all shops
and swank hotels, the office blocks & occasional
burnt out shell. So American, this destruction
& renewal, cities amnesiac where evening's

genesis falls through vast deserted silences,
towers grown otherworldly with light
thrown starlike from some alien world. Gone the Show Bar,
the Mousetrap, the whole gaudy necklace

of lacquer-dark underground lounges, halls
of mirrors, music billowing dancers
clean out of themselves beyond the dead-faced tricks,
the sick voyeurs. The Combat Zone. I can map it

in my mind, some parallel world, the ghost city
beneath the city. Parallel lives, the ones
I didn't choose, the one that kept her.
In all that dangerous cobalt luster

where was safety? Home? When we were delirium
on rooftops, the sudden thrill of wind dervishing
cellophane, the shredded cigarettes. We were
the dust the Haitians spit on to commemorate

the dead, the click & slurried fall of beads
across a doorway. In the torn & watered silk
of night, the Zone exploded its shoddy neon orchid
to swallow us in the scent of fear, emergency,

that oily street perfume & weeping brick.
Gossamer clothes, summertime and leaning
against the long dusty cars, cruising siren songs.
Summer? My memory flutters—had I—was there summer?

Dancer, and floor, and cadence
quite gathered away, and I a phantom, to you
a phantom, rehearse the story.
And now it's autumn turning hard to winter,

Thanksgiving, 1990, & all she wants is sweets
so it's apple pie barehanded & Emily's
spinning war stories, how bad she is: *So, I say,*
go ahead and shoot me, put me out of my misery.

Cut me motherfucker—my blood's gonna kill you.
Then she's too tired to sit & in the blue
kaleidoscopic tv shift I stroke
her hair, the ruined hands. *I didn't know*

how sick I was—if the heroin wanted the AIDS,
or the disease wanted the heroin. She asks me
to line up her collection of matchbox houses
so we can make a street, so we can make a neighborhood.

4. JAIL, FLAMES—JERSEY 1971

The psychic's globe whirls its winds: demons,
   countless futures, the pasts. Only
      thirteen the first time
  I saw you in jail, just a kid looking
up at me, the usual grey detective clamour,

inkpads & sodium flash. Hauled out by the officials,
   exemplary bad-news girl, they shoved
      a lyric sheet at me. Command
   recitation to sway you from straying.
"King Heroin," James Brown pompadoured like nobody's

business & here's Death cartoonishly aloft on a white
   winged horse, grim reaper lording it
      over the shivering denizens
   of a city, exaggerated as any Holy City,
going down, down, down. Just a kid, you, peering out

the jungle of your dark hair, greasy jeans, a tangle
   of beads at your throat. Ludicrous,
      I know, me declaiming within
   the jail gleam that never sleeps all over us,
that effluvium of backed up plumbing. On my palm,

the bar's iron taint lingered for hours after.
   It didn't mean that much to me, seventeen,
      my practiced sang-froid

chilling the terror, that long drop
inside, the way you collapse to fall in flames.

I might have said you'll pay for the wild & reckless hour,
   pay in the currency of sweat and shiver,
     the future squandered, the course
  of years reconfigured, relinquishment so
complete it's more utter than any falling in love. Falling

instead in flames, burning tiles spiralling to litter
   the courtyards of countless places that will
     never be yours, the fingerprints,
  tossed gloves & glittering costumes, flared
cornices & parapets, shattering panes, smoked out

or streaked with embers, the tinder of spools, such
   a savage conflagration, stupid edge-game,
     the way junkies tempt death,
  over & over again, toy with it. I might have
told you that. Everything you ever meant to be, *pfft,*

out the window in sulfured match-light, slow tinder
   & strike, possession purely ardent as worship
     & the scream working its way out
  of your bones, demolition of wall & strut
within until you're stark animal need. That *is*

love, isn't it? Everything you meant to be falls
   away so you dwell within a perfect
     singularity, a kind of saint.
  Pearl of great price. Majestic, searing,
the crystal globe spins futures unimaginable, that

crucible you know so well, Emily, viral fever refining
   you to some essence of pain more furious

than these winter trees
stripped to black nerves above
the El's streaked girders, a harsh equation, some

god's iron laughter combing down time's blind
& hush. *Hush child, forgive me.*
Twenty years later, you say
that night in jail you looked up
at me & wanted to be me. And I didn't care.

5. Address

Hello Death Angel, old familiar, old nemesis.
In the deepest hours, I have recognized
your floating shape. I've seen your breath
seduce the torn curtain
masking the empty window, have crouched with you
in the doorway, curled in the alley
hooded in your essence & shadow, have
been left blue, heart-stopped
for yours, for yours. Death,
you are the bead in the raptor's eye,
Death you dwell in the funneling depths
of the heavens beyond each
star's keening shrill, Death you are the potion
that fills the vial, the night
the monuments have swallowed. You live
in the maimed child wrapped in a wreckage
of headlines. Death you center
in the fanged oval
of the prison dog's howl. Death you dwell within
the necropolis we wake to in nightmare's
hot electric wind. You glint

the edge of the boy's razor,
patient in the blasted stairwell. Everywhere
    you walk deep lawns, tvs pollinating air
with animals wired up to dance
    for their food, with executions
& quiz shows. You're in the column
    of subway wind roaring before each
train's arrival. I've seen you drape thoughtlessly
    a woman's hair over her face
as the shot carried her forward into stop-time
    & beyond anything she'd lain
her money down for. Death your sliver works
    swiftly through the bloodstream.
Hello Death Angel, Plague is your sister.
    I've seen her handiwork, heard
the tortured breath, watched her loosen the hands
    of the dazzling boys one from each other.
For love, love. I've seen the AIDS hotels
    & sick ones begging homeless
in the tunnels, the whispered conspiracies.
    Shameless emissaries with your powders
& wands, your lunar carnivorous flowers.
    Tricks, legerdemain. I've seen you draw
veined wings over the faces of sleepers,
    the abandoned, the black feather that sweeps
so tenderly. I've seen the stain you scribe
    on the pavement, the glossy canopy of leaves
you weave. I've seen waste & ruin, know
    your kingdom for delirium, the furious thumbprints
you've scored on the flesh of those you choose.
    I've seen you slow-dance in a velvet mask, dip
& swirl across dissolving parquet.
    I've seen you swing open the iron gate—
a garden spired in valerian, skullcap, blue vervain.
    Seen you stir the neat half moons, fingernails

left absently in a glazed dish.
  Felons, I've cursed you in your greed, have spat
& wept then acquiesced in your wake. Without rue
  or pity, you have marked the lintels & blackened
the water. Your guises multiply, bewildering
  as the firmament's careless jewelry.
Death I have welcomed you to the rooms
  where Plague has lain when the struggle is passed
& lit the candles and blessed the ash.
  Death you have taken my friends & dwell
with my friends. You are the human wage.
  Death I am tired of you.

6. DARTMOUTH WOMEN'S PRISON, 1992

Emily, delirium's your province.
You dwell feverish in prison
voiceless to plead
your need before the agencies
of government who *cannot hear the buildings*
falling & oil exploding, only people walking
& talking, cannon soft as velvet from parishes
that do not know you are burning up,
that seasons have rippled
like a beast the grasses beyond
the prison.

          They cannot hear the strummed harp
of the nerves, black trees swaying winter,
cannot know your child is lost to you.

The human wage that's paid & paid?

Once, we were two girls
setting out towards that city

of endless searing night, the route taking on
the intricacy, the fumes & bafflements
of a life a woman might dream turning
feverish in her prison bunk. Probation violation,
when broke & sick, no way home
from the clinic the detective going
ride with me, just talk, that's all
I want. Twenty bucks and him crowing
we just love to run you little sluts in.

Em, if I could reach you through the dust motes'
spinning, infernoed dreams, I would dwell
in the moon's cool glistering
your cell, the rough cloth, the reflection
of your face given back in the steel basin's
water, in the smooth moan of women loving women,
a cacophony of needs. I am there with you lost
in the chaos of numbers, that nattering p.a. buzz,
in the guards' trolling clank & threat echoing
walls so eloquent
with all the high-frequency sizzle
of anguish they've absorbed.
Emily, I will bless your child, will
hold for you the bitter sponge,
would give you staff & orb, a firmament
radiant & free.

But these are phantoms, lies—
I cannot follow where you are. On my street,
the psychic's crystal globe whirls pasts, futures
but where you are is timeless.
Pain—has an Element of Blank—It cannot recollect
when it Began—or if there were
a time when it was not—
It has no Future—but itself . . .

Off the lake a toothed wind keens
& it's just me here, the one who's left.
Just me helpless to change anything caught
in this ellipsis between traffic, this
fleet human delay, all around
the wind singing like a mechanical ballerina
a girl might hold in her hand, the one
that watched your childhood bed, porcelain
upturned gaze, stiff tutu, dust in the folds
of that spindly piercing music sounding
of voices winged over water, becoming
water, & gone.

7. A STYLE OF PRAYER

There is a prayer that goes Lord I am powerless
over these carnivorous streets, the fabulous
breakage, the world's ceaseless *perpetuum mobile,*

like some renaissance design, lovely & useless
to harness the forces of weather, the planet's
dizzy spin, this plague. A prayer that asks

where in the hour's dark moil is mercy?
Ain't no ladders tumbling down from heaven
for what heaven we had we made. An embassy

of ashes & dust. Where was safety? Home?
Is this love, staff, orb & firmament?
Parallel worlds, worlds within worlds—chutes

& trapdoors in the mind. Sisters & brothers,
the same thing's going down all over town, town
after town. There is a prayer that goes Lord,

we are responsible. Harrow us through the waves,
   the runnels & lace that pound, comb, reduce us so
      we may be vessels for these stories.

Oh, the dazzling men torn one from the other,
   these women taken, these motherless children.
      Perhaps there's no one to fashion such new grace,

the world hurtling its blind proposition
   through space & prayer's merely a style of waiting
      beyond *the Hour of Lead*—

Remembered, if outlived,
   As Freezing persons, recollect the Snow—
      First Chill—then Stupor—then the letting go . . .

But Oh, let Emily become anything
   but the harp she is, too human, to shiver
      grievous such wracked & torn discord. Let her be

the foam driven before the wind over the lakes,
   over the seas, the powdery glow floating
      the street with evening—saffron, rose, sienna

bricks, matte gold, to be the good steam
   clanking pipes, that warm music glazing the panes,
      each fugitive moment the heaven we choose to make.

III

Rivers into Seas

Palaces of drift and crystal, the clouds
loosen their burden, unworldly flakes so thick
the border zones of sea and shore, the boundless zones
of air fuse to float their worlds until the spirits
congregate, fleet histories yearning into shape.

Close my eyes and I'm a vessel. Make it
some lucent amphora, Venetian blue, lip circled
in faded gold. Can you see the whorls of breath,
imperfections, the navel where it was blown
from the maker's pipe, can you see it drawn

up from the bay where flakes hiss the instant
they become the bay? Part the curtain. The foghorn's
steady, soothing moan—warning, safety, the reeling
home. Shipwreck and rescue. Stories within stories—
there's this one of the cottage nestled into dune

snowed into pure wave, the bay beyond and its lavish
rustle, skirts lifting and falling fringed in foam.
But I'm in another season—my friends' house adrift,
Wally's last spring-into-summer, his bed a raft,
cats and dogs clustered and we're watching television

floods, the Mississippi drowning whole cities
unfamiliar. How could any form be a vessel
adequate to such becoming, the stories unspooled
through the skein of months as the virus erased
more and more until Wally's nimbused as these

storm clouds, the sudden glowing ladders they let fall?
But that's not the moment I'm conjuring—it's when
my voyager afloat so many months brought back
every flood story I carried. Drifting worlds,
and Wai Min takes a shape I tell Wally as

steady watermarks across the cold bare floor—
Chinatown, South Pacific flashing its crimson,
neoned waves tranced across Wai Min's midnight eyes
behind black shades, and that voice unravelling past
each knocking winter pane. It's another world

I'm telling. Cognac and squalor. The foghorn's haunting drone
blends with that halting monotone, scarlet watermarks,
the Sinkiang's floodtides murky brown, the village
become water, swept away. Three days floating on a door,
his sister, the grandmother weaving stories endless

beneath the waxed umbrella canopy she's fashioned,
stories to soothe the children wrapped in the curtain
of her hair, to calm the ghost souls' blurred lanterns.
How rats swam to their raft, soaked cats, spirits
she said, ghosts held tranced by the storied murmurous

river. I have no spell, simply the foghorn's song
when voices unbodied, drift over water past
the low dune this cottage nestles in becoming
shape in motion stilled. No boundaries on this point,
foghorn singing its come-home incantation over

the ruthless currents. And isn't it so
we're merely vessels given in grace, in mystery,
just a little while, our fleet streaked moments?

As this day is given, singular, chilly
bolts of snow chenilled across the sky, the sea.

How to cipher where one life begins and becomes
another? Part the curtain and here's my voyager
afloat, gentle sleeper, sweet fish, dancer over
water and he's talking, laughing in
that great four-poster bed he could not leave

for months, a raft to buoy his furious radiant soul,
if I may so hazard to say that? Yes,
there was laughter, the stories, the shining dogs—
gold and black—his company. Voyager afloat
so many months, banks of sunflowers he loved spitting

their seeds. Tick. Black numerals on the sill.
A world can be built anywhere & he spun, letting go. . . .
The last time I held him, the last time we spoke, just
a whisper—hoarse—that marries now this many-voiced
    mansion
of storm and from him I've learned to slip my body,

to be the storm governed by the law of bounty given
then taken away. Shush and glide. This tide's running
high, its silken muscular tearing ruled by cycles,
relentless, the drawn lavish damasks—teal, aquamarine,
silvered steel, desire's tidal forces, such urgent

fullness, the elaborate collapse, and withdrawal
beyond the drawn curtain that shows the secret
desert of bare ruched sand. I've learned this,
I've learned to be the horn calling home
the journeyer, saying farewell. And here's

the foghorn's simple two-note wail,
mechanical stark aria that ripples
out to shelter all of us—
our mortal burden of dreams—
adrift in the sea's restless shouldering.

FOR WALLY ROBERTS, 1951–1994

Street of Crocodiles

April's chill glistens this prospect
of tarpaper roofs spreading their planes,
steam hammering pipes, mist ghosting
warming earth. In rivulets, rain casts

patterns, kaleidoscopic across windowsill
charms & artifacts. This doll,
this doll maddening with the secrecy of
her celluloid trance, rotting spirals of veil

binding her head, its trepanned crown, the disc
of skull the toymaker reached through to trigger
the lead mechanism that works her eyes. Reaches
now through the ruins, his swift gesture

seven decades gone, hands erased with the doll world
jittering its silent movies, & kinetoscopes,
maps to places that no longer exist, old empires.
Tilted, she's suddenly blind, mouth opened

as if to speak, to cry out. Hairless,
her body's evaporated to air.
The lead weight that rolls her glass eyes
hangs naked below the neck. Turn her around.

A Star of David spikes its points between
the dollmaker's initials. Below that
an oval circling *Polska*. Tilt again
and her lidless eyes resume their gaze. Lashes

and brows handpainted, exquisite, cheeks tinted
to the blush a girl might have on a chill day
gathering mushrooms. *Drive to the Vistula,*
my mother said, *the old square.* We're geomancing

for remnants. Our lost cousins found returning
with mushrooms, basketsful to wash, to hang
on strands of twine webbing their kitchen.
A lineage freighted & intricate as

these fissures across the doll's forehead,
her cheek. Irises spoked the peerless blue
of delphinium petals fallen to pale
in their dying. What fills that empty head?

Unblinking eyes that know the story?
How some made steerage & grew sleek, & the many
were left to be divided, to be dealt
the yellow cards of the murdered, to know

childhood airless breathing spiderwebs,
the must of between-the-secret-convent-walls.
To know the stopped throat of the hidden. And so
we arrived with the sheen of the spared,

& they gathered & there was much weeping,
the language unspoken for decades winging
awkward in my mother's throat. *Blood of our blood.*
Polish, shushes and wings my throat with *zimna,*

boli, glodny, rodzina. Word for cold, for pain,
the word for hunger, & for family. Lead weight
hangs in the neck, stopping the throat.
When I came home from Poland . . . I could not speak.

Ceaseless oiled glide of trains
through the tops of trees & wail of the express:
song of *we don't stop here.* But we must
linger with Stacia who gazes through my mother's

face, my own, through the kneelength drapery
of her hair. Let's begin again.
With this celluloid doll, severed head, let
her sing Orphean of her breakage, of history's

ageless demons, leather-winged swarms, colonnades
& epic monuments they contrive—Krakow's
burning cathedral whose air thickens with incense,
with whispered sins, conspiracies. Or the Kingdom

of Auschwitz with its mountains, the shorn hair
of 40,000 women turned gray by Zyklon B,
the piled cannisters & shoes, galleries
of photographs lining the walls, mute testaments

to the eloquent & terrible erasures.
The scrap of cloth, the violin case, this doll, stained
by the oils of human hands, worn by the skin.
If I hold this doll, if I drop to my knees

will something of the soul inhere? Brief
electric joys, mordant taint of fear,
something of the prayers & curses.
Empty head, all my life I've slept through dreams

that weren't my own & now we arrive again
at the place you were afraid of—the hem
of the mannequin's dress on its iron rim lufting
soft the spring air, another April, dark wine rose

among the flounces, the dress form poised
for fitting, the soup bowls left steaming
when my uncles were taken. When the children
returned, the flat mid-air, building bombed

& fragile, the bowls waited, the winds half-
forgetful lifting the rotten lace on the dress
made for a sister who would never wear it,
who left the world naked, bald. Tilt the doll,

make her blind again, the time
                        of childhood is past & over.

Though nothing's past & over. This doll's hollow skull
bears the dollmaker's touch turned to dust.
Lead weight gagging the throat & oh, to grow mute
as this celluloid head. The stuff of stiff collars,

of newsreels. Let the houselights dim, the projector's
shivering beam & we enter the *Street of Crocodiles*,
where twin filmmakers—the Brothers Quay—make
us fall through a kinetoscope to a warren

of streets, begrimed, webbed with a system
of terrible machines. Dolls with blind & numbered
heads perform their monstrous surgeries through
the murmurous river of narration, the voice

Polish, soft & dark. We are meant to think
of Mengele, of the shuddering names.
Auschwitz, Birkenau where day and night the sky
flamed vermilion and ash. A child said it was like

a movie—watching over & over the transports arrive.
Mengele waiting, the Death Angel elegant
with his white gloved hand tilting right, left,
labor or crematorium. He let the twins

keep their hair, garbed them in sailor suits,
silk dresses. Once he knelt down
and whispered to a girl, *your mother
is in that chimney, your family.*

Maybe I'll call this doll Clio after
the cruellest Muse, blank History, her pages
waiting to fill. Her mouth's perfect bow
parts—as if to cry out, as if surprised, aggrieved

at this world where Destiny, where God
has grown famous because they answer us with silence.
Her silence swarms packed as the dustmotes
in Poland, how we walked among whispers shriven

from air, lingering remnants, the unbodied shards:
a river tossed by whitecaps before the freshening
spring. A sky foaming jade, cobalt. Yellow fabric
of a dress run through the hands, the full sweet taste

of cream. Pages waiting for their ink, for
everything damned, for everything human & lovely.

Denouement

In the house, the emptied rooms, sand hushing
across bare floors, the open trunks and suitcases.

Dissolving shore, church spire and lighthouse,
we are always ready to leave, expert only

in departures, and I'm impresario
of the moment, the sky's peerless imperial

blue, combers foaming to glassy ripples
intricate as the mind, taking this all in.

Good-bye to young men strolling arm in arm,
isolate silhouettes of women glimpsed

through gauzy scarves billowing sheer
seductive semaphores. Wind off the open sea

whips the bay's wavelets to rush before it
all cresting spray. Think foaming manes

of little white mares in flight, lace froth
of a dancer's skirt lifting in the zephyr of

her arabesque gone acru into dust,
the pages of a book fanning to a whisper

tossed table to table. Berlin in 1927,
the Allaverdi's cellar club for exiles.

Now silence when the men bow towards
a shawl-draped woman who stands then sheds

her wrap. Pavlova, her career near its end.
Still she whispers to the violinist

and the crowd fades back, the drawn bow, en pointe
she sways. It could be easy now to pause,

remark the century's lunatic choreography,
or shall I go on? The drawn bow as en pointe

she sways, it's true, the final moment
of The Dying Swan. I could show her

floating, a phantom into that narrow space . . .
No, only sea breeze, these open trunks,

sand buffing the floor. I must shape elaborate
historical parallels, but her supple arms—

at hand in this spindrift instant—fishermen's
grievous bells over water, young men preening

mirrored in the shopwindows. It's simply
spring wind sculpting the bay to the lace

of a dancer's skirt and once more
I'm leaving and, just now, thought of Pavlova.

How beneath the vaulted ceiling her body sank
to the stone floor, and so like a swan's, her neck

curved smooth when the cheering crowd arose
with shadow cupped in palms before applause.

For Ann

1936–1991

The years have verdigrised the fallen leaves
on the pilgrim's monument you loved—horses'
arched necks straining towards autumn, summer's
last sultry declension. The night of the call
was the night of the planets, of gauzy cirrus
whipped, fiery seraphim cruising an atmosphere
of whispered conversations, soft alto laughter

wreathed in smoky helixes, smoke that fogged
Ann's face as she'd lean forward, a cup
held, girlish, in both hands. The night
I learned of her death, we walked
and found again that single child's ballet
slipper at shoreline. Boundaries. Water
and singing stones, day world to night world,

seasons turning one to the other, bay to open ocean.
That was the night the lacquered monkeys wove
their paws through a woman's plaited hair—
the psychic's display, and her crystal globe
of the world marked with its boundaries, winds
and demons turning silently in the window.
On that globe this night must show, the night

of the girl on the rocks tossing garlands
of freesia and dahlias, earrings into the water,
the waves' incantation, over and over, runnel
to ascent and crest, the torn lace of collapse.

The singing stones, the night the bandaged ward
shut down, morphine swaddles her riddled body.
The night somewhere, the first time, a child kickturns

in its amniotic sea, and a girl walks trailing
from her shoulders a glitter wrap so
the shadow pimps go *hey princess,*
why you so sad tonight. Freesias and dahlias
on the water, violet, rippling like a beast
in the breeze, dahlias straggling
the streets of that wooden town by the sea

where I knew her. To say, *when I knew her,*
is to say I knew something of what she dreamt
when she was young, *when she was young*
the circle skirt swept below her knees, is
to know something of her style, the gestures—
a flutter of hands. The distance intervenes.
How much is let go, what changes. . . .

The night I had the call someone had a vision
of a ballroom floating music over water.
Glenn Miller? Artie Shaw? And we walked
until the lights of the twilit boat appeared
and the music was carried over the water,
violet ripples, the turning sphere and click
slide of women slow-dancing in strapless

evening gowns, velvet masks, a world distant
from the slashed graffitied splendor of our
park. Distant as you are now, woman small
as a dancer, already half cold springtime
air, my last visit, the fierce consuming
cancer. The psychic's spinning globe
& the music of those dancing feet, your face

in April, lit with pain, & yes, apprehension
radiant above your hands' flying seraphim
attending to the sum & the glory & the flame.
Notes you'd send me pondered, stricken, composed
again on blue paper in your room with its
canopied bed, the desk with its garland
of lilies, casements opening to a garden.

To say, *I knew you.* The room empty
tonight, dust filtering its sloughed
transparent wings over the spines of books,
the neat half moons of clipped fingernails
in a glazed dish by your bed. The ballroom
floats its melodies until it's spectral,
a radiant drifting to the insect's

furious orchestra, the waves, then gone.
From whence do we come, and whither
do we go—that ancient mystery.
A crystal globe spins its provinces, the city
where your room draws its veils. Beyond
the casements, the garden's iron gate
clicks open, and who is it now that enters?

At the Westland

Life is in color, but black and white
is more real.   —Sam Fuller

The camera angle's high and dizzy:
    like a funneling throat, the elevator plunges
  down through the building.
Vertigo's intentional,
                  landing after landing
  of whispering queens, flounce
of stained organdy, velvet. Like tropical birds.

Back in the room she shares with T.,
    zoom in on faces and moons
  in cracked plaster,
                  fantastic rust continents.
The building's a hive the elevator cranks
  its tortured music through, its brass
and iron furbelows.

In the basement,
                the body waits to be found.
Spot of concrete, fish-eye view of sneaker,
laces untied, the ankle's
                  unnatural splay.
Rose patterned scarf flagged from a beltloop.

It's clear this is just another
  wasted drifter. It's clear
we're in the realm of

the assailant's blind hammer, of chemical
　　bliss that figure-eights to endlessness,
the camera impersonal
　　as the rat's onyx-eyed regard.

From the basement apartment,
　　　　　　　　　　　the Thai band
mangles the worst Rolling Stones, singer
　　wrapping his supple body round the mike,
crooning *Angie, you beautiful,*

　　　　　　　　　　crooning

with no money in our coats, dark hair
　　sweeping his lovely face, *you can't say*
we never tried. Tight close-up of the body's
hands,
　　　　a bird exploding from silk.
　　　　　　　　　　　　The band's
dreadful machinery.
　　　　　　　　The elevator's cable spooling
down, down like an antique bathysphere,
latticed iron and brass.

Long pan of the street: hotels fizzing
　　their names blue, green, rooming houses,
rundown apartment courts. Dress shop windows where
　　　mannequins cock
　　their taped and spavined wrists,

tulips shrivelling petals to show black hearts,
　　black hearts, the elevator going down.
　　　Pungent basement musk.

The pool of light its arrival throws
　　　　　　　　　　glimmers
Spider's good luck earring.
　　　Filtered, a glimpse

of the hammered face. Nothing pretty.
　　　T. saying *sweet Jesus, sweet Jesus,* while
she's flashing back through static swarming

air, the room mercuried
　　　　　　　　　in dusk, pigeon loose
and flying frantic against walls, mirror,
chilly xylophone of hangers set ringing by
its wings.
　　　　Static air.
　　　　　　　Spider taking her scarf,
her blue rose scarf. Swarming buzz. The room's

　　shades of rainwater, gunmetal, blue steel,
　　the gasoline-on-water sheen
　　　　　of the bird's feathers.
The snared bird so hot and light, its furious
　　　heart. Like an omen. This orphaned dark,

ruined door of that face, and T. going
　　I hope he was high, hope
　　he was good and high.
Beneath the skin's thin veil,
　　　　　　　her fragile bones.
　　Skitter and distortion of bad guitar, the band's
machinery terrible, *all the dreams we held so close.*
The ankle's lifeless collapse,
　　　　　　　that stacked feeling
of rooms above, hive of whispers, shrieks,
　　slaps, moans of lovemaking, dust of the building's
slow decay.
　　　　The saccharine lyrics,
　　　　　　　　tragic romance,
tragic sleep,
　　　　a song she could not hear for years

after without remembering a hive—queens primping,
   addicts twitching out on their missions. The room
she shared with T. just after
      T. stopped modelling, faces and continents
   on the walls, the thin electric hum
of power feeding the Roxie's marquee,
      jazzing evenings maracaed by platform
heels trolling down the avenue.
                              The place from which

there is no shelter. The room they shared
   like the rooms in her mind
      the basement has joined, a hive,
the door already closing. She wants to learn
      to forget. Tinny music box chords.
Where will it lead us from here?
   The shattered face.

The cost.
         Looping through reels,
                        the infinite
figure eights of film. The elevator cables'
   oiled thrum, the ride up,
      floor after black ceilinged floor, EXIT glowing
red, floor after floor.
                  Down the avenue, blackness
pools beneath parked and derelict cars,
   washes like mercury across the pavement.

From her figured scarf the bird
unfurls,
      silk and wing,
                  in flight beyond the alley's
emptied suitcases,
   the buildings' opulent parapets.
She wants to give him that. Let him have that.

Bar Xanadu

A perfect veronica, invisible, scallops air
before the bull, the bartender's fluttering hands.
Tipped with silken fruit tinselled gold,
a dusty banderilla hangs above racked bottles,
burnt-orange. Your lacquered fingers streak
the cocktail napkin and the globe of cognac's

fragrant on the zinc bar. Fields of chamomile.
Close your eyes and then the night turns to coal
seamed with diamonds. Outside, a girl murmurs
her tired price, in pesetas, to passing men.
Irita, the barman calls when she wanders in
to wash at the single cold water tap. Just a fly-blown

cafe on your functionary's street of flats, bedrooms
shuttered around their whispering, the shops that gleam
by day with scaled cellophane piglets, mounded bins
of fruit and olives. Irita rewinds her hair
at the bar, a gilt rosette nestling its waves,
tattered bullfight posters on the wall behind her

and you think of Rita Hayworth tossing roses
in *Blood and Sand,* the frayed banderilla.
Such a lovely thing to torture an animal with,
the corrida's exacting choreography
of life and death. Sometimes it's soothing to evaporate
in this smoke-patinaed air, abandoning

your imposter's life of embassy files breathing
the military names and numbers, Torrejón's

precise cold barracks. Your face wavers, oddly calm
in the mirror as the girl talks dancing and
flamenco clubs to the barman, absinthe glass shining
derangement in his hand. It's the place in the night

where you carve an uneasy confederacy
from vapor and exhaustion, a trio—the alien,
the clownish poseur, the girl with nothing to sell
but herself and straitened, cataleptic dreams.
She stretches, plays idly the slot machines
spinning roses, babies and lemons, the brilliant

suit of lights. The caramel glow of the barlamps haloes
her hair, bitten lips. Another sip and the slots'
click is rosary beads wafting prayers up
to a heaven of slink and spangle, quick bargains
struck in alcoves, that old palm of chapped fingers
slipping coins to the gas meter, of spreading stain

across the counterpane. Around Bar Xanadu
narrow streets fill with the violet steam
of after-midnight, the pigeon's soft veneral
cooing that speaks of want like this, that deep
original loneliness. There are heartless places
in every city you've lived. Cognac spreads

its window of warmth and the drifting years return
bordered with the crimes of night, with cramped
rooms you've climbed to, dead as the money
in your pockets. A "dimestore Mata Hari,"
the bureau chief called you while he snipped
a fresh cigar. On parched plains outside the city

soldier boys drill before the fighter planes, glamorous
with starlight, still floating half-sleep

in some Iowa of vinyl booths and Formica, miles
of hissing corn. But it's closing hour and beneath
your fingers the napkin snows its raddled lace
across the bar and you must rise with them, rise

to dust with the barman his green bottle, help him
to don the sparkling jacket. Rise to strap
the magic shoes to Irita's feet
and then you must walk with her these streets
you'll never leave, gritty with wind from Andalusia
riffling your skirt in the scent of blood oranges and sweat.

Fortunate Traveller

Dazed and voluptuous, Monroe sways through
the casino towards Gable. The last film.
Her soft face, like her voice, breathless
above subtitles, the Spanish premiere

of *The Misfits,* thirty years late. The line had wound
the block beneath a sky, stagy
and ultramarine, swept with klieg lights,
sherried autumn air. Like a trapdoor opening

in time, ladders and tunnels, the metro's
black underground wind beneath the theater,
blue signal flash. Each platform's arched and tiled, columned
and inscribed, resplendent as memory palaces

monks once constructed, lavish scriptoriums
of the mind for arcane texts, scrolls and histories.
I'd wanted to hear American voices, the velvet
curtained hush framing spectacular faces.

Los Perdidos, the translation skews, the clement
darkness violined as the stars navigate
tawdry celluloid orbits through the bungled script
of drifters whose luck dissolves at desert's edge.

Tossed dollar bills crisp around her ankles,
Monroe shimmies, the barroom scene, hair musical, those
naked humid eyes. Houselights, dim, benevolent.
This morning, the Opera stop's electric

no-time, then the metro's plunge into the tunnel.
    Swaying from the handgrip on the way from
the doctor, his ancient fluoroscope that verdigrised
    everything it touched, my reflection rippled,

        insubstantial in the coal-blacked pane, tangled in
layers of reflection, circus posters tumbling
        half-naked spangled acrobats pentimentoed
    across the glass. Everyone I talk to these days

        is both here and not here, entranced by leaf-smoke,
        coal-smoke. Anthracite, the blue enduring flame.
Bituminous, yellow flame, burning quickly,
        volatile. Billowing tobacco clouds, the audience

        fans programs and onscreen the chemistry fails to
ignite but for this love scene, tender and confused,
        between Clift and Monroe. The alley outside the bar.
    They'd kept forgetting their lines, passing between takes

    a silver flask of vodka, washing down
        barbiturates until finally the shooting stopped
and that's why the scene's so lost. *Los Perdidos.*
    Crimson Seconals, the Tuinals and canary-yellow

    Nembutals, the stoked hues of leaves dervished in the
        parks'
dry fountains, sherried autumn air. Like trapdoors in time,
        a yeasty breeze redolent as the breeze shaking
    winged maples in the park by the railroad station,

    the group of friends I had when I was young.
        Another city. Of all that group, I alone

am left to glimpse beneath these actors' faces
        other faces, behind Monroe's hand steadying

                herself on the torn car seat this hand fluoroscoped
green and fleshless, all arthritic whorls and ratchets,
            to see in those fanned bones the *transi*'s hand, caught
        between life and afterlife, carved above

            the sandstone archway in the ruined monastery
                garden near our flat, already part of memory's
cluttered gallery. Here is the urn that holds
        the lover's ashes, the harp that plays

                the friend's delirium, the coal brazier measuring
time: anthracite burning blue, enduring, bituminous
            sulfur flames, the quick ones, black-bordered
    postscripts,
        those mistakes smudging police blotters. Of all that
group

            I'd meet when I was young: a trapdoor opening in
    time—
                this one of the russet curls blown across a pale
    forehead,
this one I loved, rich laughter from a black throat like
        no other, the spark and groan of trains braking at

                the little station. Translation fails. The metro rumbles
beneath the theater as Los Perdidos reel suffused by
            harsh mineral desert glow. When the last
        shot of the actress's gone lovely face furls away,

        I alone will taste the foreign coffee, sweet
            and thick. I alone shall watch these hands vanish

in bewildering autumnal smokes, an evening
at this century's end when wrought-iron streetlamps

print wands and serifs over everything
they suffer to touch.
Of all that group I'd meet when I was young . . .
I can't recall what we spoke of—it meant so much.

The Window

Streak of world blurred charcoal & scarlet, the El slows,
brakes at the platform, Little Chinatown,
& there's that window, peeling frame, screen split

to rippling raingusts. A curtain breathes
through busted glass, a glimpse of hallway
enamelled green, rows of numbered doors, nothing more,

and then the train lurches forward sparkling
its electric signature above slick, hissing rails.
Soon, soon, I'll stop there, the window's pull

irresistible as the force of a star collapsed
to black gravity. I'll step through the window,
take up again the key for the one room to which

I keep returning. Let me wait again there by the sill
as I wait still. Here's the steeple of the burnt church,
beloved of vandals, the sooty block of

old law tenements where chipped tubs rise
porcelain on their feet in cold-water kitchens,
unashamed, small gray animals, the startled

array of insects we lived with.
Where are you? In the hallways, bodies passing
smell like bodies, unwashed, ginsoaked, dopesick,

the musk & salt. Where are you?
Hear with me the slant beat of that orthopedic shoe
striking pavement a few stained facades away.

With each echoing step, feel again the raw acceleration,
hope, or is it fear looming, receding?
Steaming hellmouths in the asphalt. If each of us

contains, within, humankind's totality, each possibility
then I have been so fractured, so multiple & dazzling
stepping towards myself through the room where

the New Year's dragon lies in its camphored sleep.
In the days I lived here, a thousand rooms
like it, making love was a way of saying *yes,*

I am here, these are my borders, hold me down
a little while. Make me real to myself. One more shining
thing gone after in the night that disappeared

with morning. No substance. But I'd like you
to place your hands, cradling the neck's swanny
arch, stand here by the copper dormer window

that's like an endless gallery of such windows
with fire escapes burdened by doves' insatiable
mourning. Then let it happen, the desire to be out

in the world, more than in it, wholly of it,
trammelled, broken to neoned figments.
All it takes is a few adjustments—

purple those lids, the lips as we did then,
that old mirror clouded with vague continents. We're
ready to inhabit the sequinned gowns, martini glasses

pouring their potions over the street, the milky syringes
& oh, those ravening embraces, the ravished streets
& whispered intersections. Slick back

the hair, and then the wig. I could never face anything
without the wig. Transformed, the old vaudeville desire
struts & kicks its satiny legs, the desire to be

consumed by ruined marquees, these last drifting hotels,
to be riven, served up singing, arched & prismed
from a thousand damp boulevards. Those things which shine

in the night, but what vertigo to surrender, falling
through the elaborate winged buildings they only have
in neighborhoods like this anymore, January's bitten snow

cold about the ankles. Let me move again, a wraith,
past these windows—bridesmaids' gowns the color
of casket linings, flammable, green

as gasoline poured from the can to flame the alley
outside the Welfare's fluorescent offices,
police stations, the shabby public hospital's endless

waiting rooms. How exactly pinned-to-the-wall
love was in that harsh economy, the world, the world, the
    world.
What I remember is the astringent sting of air.

Living on nothing but injections & vodka, a little
sugar. The self, multiple, dazzling. What I remember
are the coral husks of lobsters broken clean

through restaurant windows, steaming. Through these
windows tumble fragments, the stories, lavish
vertical fountains of opera. Dressed as death's-heads,

crowds demonstrate against the new war
with placards before the marble stairs. Like a wraith
let me move again among them, through the rooms

of this building, home of my fondest nightmares, let me
stay the hand twisting in rage, let me crush
the white & violet petals of sleep, the black sticky heart

of sleep over the delicate eyelids, over the bodies'
soft geographies, over the sorrow, the grandeur
of columns & esplanades, the soot-shouldered graces

outside the museum. Rude armfuls of orchids
fill the florist's windows, these lunar ones
curved like music staffs above dissolving aspirins

I might bring back to the room for you. Oh phantoms.
Oh the many lives that have fountained through
my own. Soon, soon, I shall stop upon that platform

& you will meet me there, the world rosegray beyond
the scalloped tops of buildings & we shall seek
that thing which shines & doth so much torment us.

Afterword

James Merrill once noted—famously—Elizabeth Bishop's "instinctive, modest, life-long impersonation of an ordinary woman." My friend Lynda Hull spent her life impersonating an extraordinary woman. Perhaps *personate* might be a better verb; it's not that anything about the performance was false but that Lynda was devoted to the creation of a self, on the page and off. Her artifice, her maquillage—literal and verbal—were not disguises but part of a quest for the authentic. Like the drag performers she loved, Lynda understood that the authentic self is not necessarily the naked one; we forge ourselves as we forge poems, out of the materials at hand: our histories, the stuff of character and circumstance, all the occasions of style. Style, at its highest, is not decoration but a gesture of revelation; surface can be, when most deliberate, most consciously wrought, what John Ashbery called someplace "a visible core."

Are all identities forgeries, in the sense of made things? Don't we "forge" ourselves, in the work of soul-making? How many selves can we come to embody, to personate? "If each of us / contains, within," Lynda wrote,

> humankind's totality, each possibility
> then I have been so fractured, so multiple & dazzling
> stepping towards myself through the room where
>
> the New Year's dragon lies in its camphored sleep.
> In the days I lived here, a thousand rooms
> like it, making love was a way of saying *yes,*
>
> *I am here, these are my borders, hold me down*
> *a little while. Make me real to myself.*

("The Window")

The self Lynda would make real would not suffice were it not remarkable. In the difficult time since her death in March of 1994—in an automobile accident, on a wet winter road in Massachusetts—I have found myself beginning to focus not so much on that loss, enormous as it is, as on exactly how much Lynda accomplished, in her thirty-nine years, and what a legacy she leaves behind, in her three volumes of poems. No poet of my generation seems to me more remarkable, more irreplaceable.

Lynda and I were friends for a decade, so I can suggest only a little of what passed between us. We were writers with a common spirit—sometimes, it seemed, a common blood. She was for me—as I know was also the case for other writer friends of hers—both the sharpest and the most sympathetic of my critics. Her work always pushed me forward, suggesting how much further there was to go, how deeply the world of the poem might be entered, how much more finely wrought its language might become. Her absolute dedication to work—work as anchor, discipline, calling, as a steady act of attention—both humbled and prodded.

And we were colleagues, her devotion to her teaching demonstrating how transformative the exchanges between teacher and student might be. Lynda poured herself into her teaching with the kind of energy and passion brought to it only by people who themselves feel the vulnerability and uncertainty of their students. Such teachers have a powerful desire to receive what they know how to give: witness, faith, courage. I've never known a teacher to inspire such ardor in her students, a desire to be not like Lynda but like themselves—to step into their authority, *their* defining costume.

And we were, lastly, as straight woman to gay man, girlfriends, a bond which is not to be thought of superficially but can—like matters of style—come close to the bone. Confidants, sisters, fellow bitches, we could both dish and cry our eyes out together. Sometimes she'd describe herself as "a gay man trapped in a woman's body," and I can't think of Lynda without, indeed, thinking of the accomplishment of her sartorial style: turban, jet earrings, leopard-spotted scarf, the angular and aubergine coif. This is no mere matter of decor. Style, of course, conceals and reveals—that is what style is for—and Lynda seems to me now a seamless creation; her clothes, like her poetry, alive with nerve and glamour, her glitter allied with her vulnerability, a characteristic alloy of strength and damage.

My lover and I bought her a black beaded dress, at an auction, a sheer black breath of a thing redolent of jazz, dissipation, and a whiff of sin. It was so small, and so entirely right for Lynda's character, that I doubt anyone else in the world could have worn it. She wore it to the ballroom of the Plaza, in Manhattan, on one of our last nights together, accessorized with long jet earrings and a gleaming ebony cane. That time—and the years from which these poems arise—was a period of enormous difficulty. A trip to Poland with her mother awakened a deep sense of grief at the loss of ancestry, a profound sense of horror. Then, after her first automobile accident—her car struck by a taxi in Chicago, her feet and ankles shattered—Lynda was physically never the same, living in continuous pain. And a season in Cambridge, in 1993, brought a welling up of memory, a struggle with the shadows of early years in Boston. But that evening all the year's struggle was subsumed somehow, transformed in the dark sparkle of her self-presentation. In her dress and cane, she seemed to be of a piece with all her own passions: Hart Crane, Joseph Cornell, Chet Baker, the intersections of glamour and trash, fake leopard skin, marcasite, rhinestones, wigs, violet pastilles which came in silvery deco wrappers and were available only in New Jersey, trains, hotels, film noir, hats with veils.

What Lynda wore, above all else, was her own past. She inhabited it like that spangled wraith of a dress, only less comfortably; it was heavy and inescapable, a source of both pain and glory. She had survived a difficult life, of addictions and trouble in "the ghost city / beneath the city." It's amazing that she became what she was—a writer and teacher—but astonishing that she became *who* she was, a poet of compelling, undeniable power and vision. It wasn't supposed to happen. Alcohol, heroin, the streets' ruthless machinery all said so. But Lynda, consummate survivor, fortunate traveler, had ideas of her own, and a furious will. Though however she'd remake herself, the past was a sort of huge wardrobe she dragged about with her, and though she was always ready to travel—one eye always on the escape route—what she carried was immense, unmanageable.

The past—our individual account with grief—is to be neither romanticized nor escaped. If the difficulty of personal history is glamorized, in these poems, it is because glamor is a way of making history bearable. The wigs gleam, the rhinestones tremble while the harsh gears of the world go on grinding. But the beautiful gestures of aspiration *shine*—even if their context is bitter, tawdry, or unforgiving. Perhaps these gleam more brilliantly— certainly more chillingly—because they are set against so much dark.

"I was always," said Billie Holiday on her deathbed, "a religious bitch." The credo might have been Lynda's own. The religion of the poems is aesthetic; they worship in the church of Hart Crane and Proust—may I add Chanel? But their mission is ethical as well, since they are after redemption. What, in our harrowed and harrowing cities, can be held up as lovely, genuine, human? The stories her poems tell are often brutal ones, narratives of lost or shattered lives, and yet her language is never diminished or blunted. She is as involved with how the story is to be told as with the story itself, as if the way in which the words are hammered out will make the terror of the tale acceptable, for a while, will contain it. Style, for Lynda, was redemptive work. If the stories of a life cannot be changed, they can be honored, polished, set into the beautiful vitrines and *retablos* of a radiant poetics. Like Joseph Cornell, Lynda arranged the stuff of memory and longing into settings whose beauty underlines the elegiac nature of what is contained. The box is an act of mourning, a stay against time and disappearance, but its allure is permeated by loss. Penny arcades, Times Square movie palaces, the Manhattan skyline shaped like antique radios: places a lonely man from Queens or a desperate girl from Newark might turn for transcendence.

In the end, the poems of *The Only World* are poems of survival. They bear the stamp of testimony, the testament of one who experiences herself as the only living witness. "Of all that group, I alone/am left," she tells us in "Fortunate Traveller." *Only I lived to tell.* How many of us feel this way now? Who else knows what we do, who else will carry our dead, or tell their stories, when there are so many? "Oh the many lives," she writes, "that have fountained through/my own."

The pain of the last years of Lynda's life was, for her, a source of connection to the suffering of her times. Our century's great accumulating losses seemed continuous; from the Holocaust to the burning of Newark to the epidemic, what was erased was her *family*, her context. The poems track the terrifying passage of having seen it all, remembered everything, turned from nothing. Lynda did not live, but she did—and does—live to tell; she hammered out for herself something we cannot lose: a voice essential, dynamic, unmistakable. She was a "fortunate traveller" in that she was not numbed, not overcome by those forces, external or internal, that would silence her. One response to horror—in Poland or Newark or Provincetown—is silence. Another is to make what one can, to create with all the more ardor and fury. I think now of that frail and compromised body, so carefully clothed in a survivor's bravura gestures. Just so the poems: lustrously, complexly layered, their diction gorgeously burnished, syntax unrolling like reels of film.

I wish that Lynda were here to wear the beaded dress to celebrate the publication of this book, which merits and requires our dressing up, in our grandest clothes—not only to celebrate its triumph but also to stave off its chill, intractable darkness. We buried the dress with her. Now my friend's only jewels are these lapidary phrases, in their terrifying and glittering cascades—

fixed now, historical. Her costume, her signifying surface, is like the red velvet jacket she evokes in one of these poems:

> the shade of flame offering its drapery, its charm
> against this world burning ruthless, crucial & exacting.

MARK DOTY

About the Author

Lynda Hull was born in Newark, New Jersey, in 1954, and was the author of two previous collections of poetry, *Ghost Money*, which was published by the University of Massachusetts Press in 1987 as that year's winner of the Juniper Prize, and *Star Ledger*, which appeared from the University of Iowa Press in 1991 as winner of the Edwin Piper Memorial Prize. She was the recipient of fellowships from the National Endowment for the Arts, the Illinois Arts Council, the Carl Sandburg Book Award (for *Star Ledger*), and three Pushcart Prizes. Her poems appeared in many journals and anthologies, among them *The New Yorker, Poetry, Best American Poetry, The Kenyon Review, The Iowa Review, Ploughshares, New England Review, Agni Review*, and *The Gettysburg Review*. She taught at Johns Hopkins University, Indiana University, De Paul University, Brandeis University, and in the MFA in Writing Program of Vermont College. *The Only World* was completed shortly before her death in 1994.